Joseph's Execution

Dr Dhieu Mathok Diing Wol

Translated by
Dr Muhammad Farpuq Badr
Nuha Muhammad Omran

The publisher wishes to acknowledge and thank Dr. Douglas H. Johnson for his invaluable help and support for Africa World Books and its mission of preserving and promoting African cultural and literary traditions and history. Dr. Johnson and fellow historians have been instrumental in ensuring that African people remain connected to their past and their identity. Africa World Books is proud to carry on this mission.

ISBN: 9781763873469

Cover design, typesetting and layout: Africa World Books
Unit 3, 57 Frobisher St, Osborne Park, WA 6017
P.O. Box 1106 Osborne Park, WA 6916

Africa
World Books
Pty Ltd

Contents

To the souls of the innocent Victims of apartheid,

ethnic and religious discrimination.

Introduction

The Assassination of Justice in "Joseph's Execution"

We have come to know Dr. Dhieu Mathok Diing Wol as a distinguished politician, academic and researcher of the highest calibre. In addition to currently serving as the Minister of Investment in the Republic of South Sudan, although not a professional novelist who writes literature for its own sake, he uses this novel "Joseph's Execution" to deliver a clear societal and humanitarian message.

Being a reader and a publisher, it was a pleasant surprise for me when Dr. Wol chose to send the manuscript of this novel to Al-Nokhba Publishing House for publication and requested that I write a critical perspective on its Arabic version.

From the very first lines of "Joseph's Execution", it became clear that Dr. Wol had chosen the art of storytelling as a window to express the injustices and loss of justice caused by apartheid, ethnic and religious discrimination, which ultimately leads to the tragic loss of innocent lives.

As I continued reading, I could imagine Dr. Wol, a man often characterised by his calls for love, tolerance, and peace, pouring his anger against racism and persecution of all forms into this narrative.

The story of Joseph, unjustly imprisoned for years and sentenced to execution for an absurd and incomprehensible reason, is a powerful medium of expression. Joseph bore the consequences of a murder he did not commit, merely because people in Khartoum had misidentified him as "Yusuf" instead of his real name, "Joseph".

Perhaps this absurdity is what drove Dr. Wol to abandon

his usual calm demeanour and boldly reject the injustices of a period in Sudan's history, starting from Omar al-Bashir's 1989 coup. This era saw Sudan exploited by terrorist organisations and internationally wanted individuals, resulting in class violence, persecution of minorities, and the displacement of many South Sudanese from their ancestral lands.

The narrative explores the tragedy of Joseph, born into a conservative family connected to traditional authority. During the Southern Sudan rebellion in the late 1970s, his village in Northern Bahr Al-Ghazal faced militia raids, livestock was stolen, women and children were abducted, villages were burned and the spoils were transported to Darfur, Kordofan, and sometimes to White Nile region.

Desperately, after his family losing their cattle, Joseph fled to Khartoum in search of a new life. He left his home in Majok Diing Wol for Ariath, a small town on the railway in Northern Bahr Al-Ghazal, to catch a train. Unbeknownst to him, this journey would be the last of his life.

Despite the story's angry tone against apartheid and religious discrimination, Dr. Wol's narrative consistently reflects moments of tolerance, peace, and love. These themes emerge, especially in instances where Muslims protected their Christian brothers from persecution, often at great personal cost.

This was particularly evident in an exchange between Father Emmanuel Franco and Sergeant Osman from Kober Prison. When Joseph requested a priest to pray for him before his execution, Father Emmanuel asked Osman, "Are you a Christian?"

Osman replied, "Not at all. I'm Muslim."

The priest then inquired, "Why are you so concerned about this?"

Osman answered, "Because Joseph is innocent and all religions, including Islam, stand against injustice."

Through this, the author conveys a powerful message: religious persecution, apartheid, and injustice are not rooted in the essence of religions but in the practices of individuals and groups claiming to speak for God. Such negative phenomena plunge society into deep moral, political, and social decline.

The dialogues in "Joseph's Execution" are written in simple Sudanese colloquial dialect, making the story relatable, as if the reader were watching a cinematic film. This simplicity makes it easy to envision the work as a compelling cinematic adaptation, immortalising the story of a young man who lost his life for no crime of his own, but being mistaken for someone else.

The author skillfully integrates Sudan's dramatic political developments into the narrative. Although some traditional critics might argue that this novel doesn't adhere to classical fiction, it provides a sharp critique of a turbulent historical era in the Sudan:

> *It cannot be definitively stated that the deterioration of justice began during Al Bashir's era, as there were early signs hinting at the erosion of the rule of law and the collapse of the constitutional order during Al-Sadiq Al-Mahdi's tenure, owing to the civil war in the country. This was most evident in the south, east, Darfur, the Nuba Mountains, and Blue Nile regions.*

On the morning of Friday, June 30, 1989, unusual movements began inside Kober Prison, where significant figures in Sudanese politics were brought to detention.

The prison administration requested that some cells be vacated for the new detainees. Those accused of murder, whose sentences were nearly completed were relocated to the new cells and Joseph was transferred into Cell No. 9.

The following day, Hassan Al-Turabi and Sadiq Al-Mahdi arrived at Kober Prison. It was said that Al-Turabi's detention was a staged act by the Islamists to conceal their involvement in the military coup. Numerous ministers, parliamentarians and senior military officers were also detained."

Hence, I see that "Joseph's Execution" represents a model of the political novel which exposes the flaws of governance based on false religious pretences that impoverished Sudan and its people for decades. The novel can be fairly seen as an expression of a real crisis of that entire period of time.

Being hanged to death would be the most tragic end for an innocent young man who paid his life for nothing but being named "Yusuf" instead of his real name "Joseph".

In the end, Joseph had no choice but to entrust his jailer

with his final wish to inform his family of the truth. As the author writes:

The family of the late Joseph John agreed to close this case and refrain from raising the issue. They prayed for divine justice and for his soul to rest in peace. Still, recounting this story, as detailed in his will, became a promise to the living, a tale that had to be told for him to find eternal solace.

- Osama Ibrahim
- Media Professional and Director of Al-Nokhba Publishing House

Chapter One

Overwhelmed with extreme sadness, the prison guard, Sergeant Osman Khater Adam, enters Cell No. 9. He delivers a poignant message to the prisoner, Joseph John Bak, known as "Yusuf", who has been sentenced to death by hanging.

"Joseph, the administration has granted you permission to visit your relatives," he says, his voice loaded with emotion.

This was to be the last visit in his life before being taken to the gallows at dawn the next day. This emotional message reaches Joseph at approximately 4:00 pm after spending over six years in Kober Prison in Khartoum Bahri, having served a ten-year sentence for his inability to pay blood-money amounting to twenty-one thousand Sudanese pounds.

Joseph leaves his cell, accompanied by Sergeant Osman and another guard, heading to the house of his uncle, the retired General Morris Tong, a former governor of the Bahr el-Ghazal region. His uncle's home is located in Al-Taif, one of the upscale neighbourhoods of Khartoum. Joseph's mother and General Morris are cousins from the Pashiermeth sub-clan of Northern Bahr el Ghazal.

As they walk, Joseph's mind races. He has only one dream in the few remaining hours of his life: to inform his uncle that he was not guilty and was not the killer. Rather, he was a victim of Sudan's Islamic Civilisational Project. He accepts his fate, believing in the will of the Creator as long as he was innocent. Therefore, he wants to ask his uncle, General Morris, to convey this truth to his family, especially his mother, Teresa. He believes that speaking out the truth will free him from his sins and burdens, including his encounter with Osama Bin Laden and his conversion to Islam.

"I need to tell him the truth, Osman," Joseph says, his voice trembling. "I need him to know I didn't do it."

"I know, Joseph," Osman replies softly. "Let's hope he's home."

Joseph's shoulders slump as he stares at the empty house. Another misfortune—no, a curse— to add to the litany of his life: the raided cattle, the militias at Atokthou, the blood-money he could never pay.

Joseph learns from his cousin at the house that his uncle is away on a family visit to a sick relative at Bahri Teaching Hospital.

The other prison guard who is accompanying them looks at his watch. "We need to return to the prison, Osman. It's getting late," he says.

"I'm sorry, Joseph," Osman says, placing a comforting hand on his shoulder. "We have to go back."

At 3:00 am, guards shackle Joseph's wrists. His feet drag against the cold stones as they march him to the gallows, where the noose swings like an hourglass, counting his final seconds.

His body was buried in the Muslim cemetery in Al-Sahafa without the knowledge of anyone from his family.

2.

Joseph was born into a conservative family deeply rooted in traditional leadership. His father served as the omada (junior chief) of the Patek clan, a respected clan in the village, particularly in regard to African beliefs and communal arbitration during crises or natural disasters. However, the sudden attacks by raiding nomads were beyond the control of these traditional beliefs, especially as the younger generation, including Joseph, had abandoned the old ways and converted to Christianity. This shift rendered the clan ineffective in addressing calamities as they once had.

By the late 1970s and during the early days of the rebellion in Southern Sudan, the frequency of attacks by militias (Popular Defence Forces) and the Murahilin (a term also used for the Janjaweed in South Darfur and West Kordofan) increased. These assaults targeted villages along the railway line, particularly in northern Bahr el-Ghazal. Areas like Atokthou, Korok, Duluit, Peth-Atak, and Ayat in Aweil North suffered immensely.

These areas adjoined the Rizeigat, Habaniya, and Misseriya tribes near Abiem in Aweil East. Organised militia raids devastated these villages, looting cattle, abducting women and children, and burning homes. The stolen properties and goods were often transported to Darfur, Kordofan, or even to the White Nile region.

Despairing over the loss of their cattle and the resulting hardship, Joseph decided to head north to Khartoum in search of a new life. He chose this path instead of following his peers to Ethiopia, where many joined the rebellion at Bilpham to obtain firearms for defending their homeland.

Joseph departed his home in Majok Diing Wol village for Ariath, a small town on the railway line connecting Wau and Babanusa in Western Kordofan. From there, he planned to board a train. Unbeknownst to him, this journey would be his last departure, with no return.

Before heading north, Joseph spent a few days with his aunt Mary in her home on the western side of the town. Her house faced the railway from the east, with the bustling Ariath market behind it and the famous livestock market nearby. The memory of their cattle being looted haunted

Joseph, surfacing every time he saw cows. He decided not to inform his aunt about his plans to travel north, fearing her opposition to the idea.

The train, locally known as the "Aweil Train", made its weekly journey from Babanousa to Wau, passing through Aweil. Although Wau was its southernmost stop, many passengers bound for northern Sudan boarded it, especially those from greater Gogrial. Over time, the train became synonymous with Aweil.

At 8:00 pm, the train arrived in Ariath. Joseph boarded it secretly, leaving his relatives behind. By dawn, he found himself in Babanousa. Short on funds for the rest of his journey to Khartoum, he decided to stay in Babanousa temporarily to make enough money.

Joseph found work with a cart owner, delivering drinking water to homes—a lucrative job compared to other menial tasks in the city. The cart owner offered him twenty-five percent of the daily earnings, a generous share that allowed him to save for his trip while covering his living expenses. Joseph decided to work there for three months before continuing to Khartoum.

While in Babanousa, Joseph befriended Martin, a man from Atokthou who had left five years earlier.

Joseph said one evening as they shared a meal, "I heard you will be going to Khartoum, Martin."

"Yes Joseph, it has been a long time here in Babanousa since I left home."

"I hope Khartoum will be different," said Joseph.

"It will be, Joseph, because it is a big city neither like Ariath nor Babanousa," Martin replied. "When there, stay focused and work hard and you'll achieve your dream." Martin added.

Joseph nodded and said, "You are right, Martin."

"I'm planning to travel to Khartoum next week." Martin announced, "Ok That's good news, Martin, because I have a letter to my relative in Al-Lamab to inform them that I'm coming in the week after." Joseph declared his intention to travel too.

"That's fine, Joseph," Martin agreed to deliver the letter.

A week later, Joseph reached the Al-Shajara's train station, the penultimate stop before Khartoum. This station, close to Al-Lamab, was less crowded than Khartoum's main terminal. Joseph's relatives awaited him at the station and welcomed him warmly. They brought him to their home, the very house where he would later be arrested for murder and face the prospect of execution.

Most of the young men in this household worked in marginal jobs, such as domestic servants (commonly referred to as Ochin), municipal workers, or porters at the Sajana market. Others worked in factories, especially those producing soft drinks like Pepsi, Coca-Cola, and Mirinda. Initially, Joseph joined the group working at the Sajana market before securing a position at the Pepsi-Cola factory. He spent over six months there, hauling heavy loads of steel, cement, and zinc.

Despite being new to the city, Joseph quickly earned a reputation for his kindness and good manners. This respect led his colleagues and the local merchants to give him the nickname "Yusuf", a name derived from his original name, Joseph. This nickname reflected the shared history of Joseph in Christianity—St. Joseph, the betrothed of Mary, mother of Jesus—and Yusuf in Islam, the prophet revered in both religions.

3.

Almost every evening at 7:00 pm, Mohiy Al-Din returned home from the club with his younger brother, Nasr Al-Din. One fateful night, as they pushed open the gate, they froze: two strangers were desecrating the family portraits displayed by the main gate, urinating on the framed faces of their ancestors.

"What in God's name are you doing?" Mohiy roared, his voice cracking with fury.

The men didn't flinch. One even smirked, still relieving himself on the photograph of Mohiy's late grandfather. Mohiy charged forward, fists balled. "Look at me when I'm speaking to you!"

The blade came too fast to dodge. A glint of steel, a wet gasp, and Mohiy crumpled to the dirt, clutching his chest. Blood seeped between his fingers as he stared up at his killer—a hollow-cheeked man with wild eyes.

"Why'd you kill him, Yusuf?" the second man whimpered, backing away.

"Shut up and run!" the one referred to as Yusuf hissed.

They vanished westward, toward the labyrinth of mudbrick homes where Joseph— nicknamed Yusuf—lived with his family.

Hearing his son's cries, Sheikh Ahmed Sharif, Mohiy's father, rushed out of the house to the scene, only to find that his son had already passed away.

"What happened?" he demanded, his voice breaking.

Struggling through tears, Nasr replied, "Mohiy is dead, father…" He broke into uncontrollable sobs, clutching his head.

The father, visibly shaken, asked, "Tell me what happened, Nasr."

"We found two men urinating on the wall. When we confronted them, one of them stabbed Mohiy in the chest. The other asked the killer, 'Why did you kill the man, Yusuf?' Then they ran westward."

The father sighed deeply and said, "There is no power or strength except with Allah, the Almighty. We entrust ourselves to Allah's justice."

Nasr Al-Din echoed the father's invocation, and then went inside to call the police. The authorities arrived at the scene, transported the body to the morgue, and began filing a case against an unknown assailant, noting that the suspect was referred to as Yusuf.

Mohiy Al-Din was a final-year law student at the University of Cairo's Khartoum branch, just two months away from graduation. His untimely death left his family in profound grief, especially his mother, who was already battling hypertension and diabetes.

Sheikh Ahmed Sharif, a prominent Islamic figure and head of the neighbourhood's religious group, frequently organised large rallies in the public square near his house, attended by leaders of the Islamic movement, including Sheikh Hassan Abdullah al-Turabi, whose party formed part of the opposition during the Third Democracy.

The criminal investigations department at the Al-Lamab Police Station formed teams to pursue the case, focusing on individuals named "Yusuf" across the neighbourhood and South Khartoum. Under pressure from the family and the Islamic movement, suspicion fell on Joseph John Bak, also known as Yusuf.

One day, three police officers arrived at the Pepsi-Cola

Company with an arrest warrant for someone named Yusuf. They discovered he was on medical leave, so they went to his residence, arrested him, and took him to the Al-Lamab Police Station for interrogation on charges of murder. The case had no witnesses except the victim's brother, Nasr Al-Din, who was present during the incident near their home. He could not identify the attacker, except for the phrase spoken by the accomplice: "Why did you kill the man, Yusuf?" This phrase aligned with the nickname Yusuf, given to Joseph by traders and colleagues in the Sajana market.

The victim's family was determined to pin the crime on Joseph. They pushed for a police lineup, where Joseph was the only Southerner among a group of Northerners. This setup played into the deep-seated stereotype that Southerners were prone to criminality—an unspoken bias that had long influenced social and legal judgments in the North. Under the poor visibility of the 7:00 pm incident, shrouded in near-total darkness, Nasr Al-Din's identification of Joseph seemed inevitable. His eyes scanned the lineup, and whether consciously or instinctively, they landed on the lone Southerner. In a society conditioned to associate Southerners with violence and lawlessness, Joseph became the obvious, if not the only, suspect. The accusation was not just a matter of memory—it was shaped by prejudice, and in that moment, Joseph's fate was sealed.

He was immediately handcuffed, detained, and charged with premeditated murder under Article 251 of the 1984 *Penal Code*. In 1991, following the Islamist coup led by Brigadier Omer Hassan Ahmed Al-Bashir, the law was amended and the Article changed to 130, introducing harsher penalties for murder—further tightening the grip of an already unjust system on individuals like Joseph, who were vulnerable to its biases.

4.

The uphill task for Joseph's family was to hire a lawyer to defend him in this fabricated case. However, this was incredibly difficult, given the family's dire financial situation. Most of the family members, having lost their livestock to looters in the area, were left penniless. Some had moved to Khartoum, where they worked in marginal professions, such as municipal labourers, company workers, or porters in marketplaces.

Yet, Joseph's good reputation among his acquaintances, particularly the owners of lumberyards and shops in Sajana, prompted many to contribute significant amounts toward his defence, as everyone knew he was innocent.

"We have to help Joseph," one of his colleagues at the Pepsi-Cola factory said. "He's a good man. We can't let him face this alone." A notable role was also played by his colleagues in Sajana Market and the Pepsi-Cola Company, who rallied to raise the necessary funds for legal fees.

News of the court case reached lawyer Babiker through one of Joseph's relatives, who worked at his house as a gate-keeper. Deeply moved by the injustice, Babiker volunteered to defend the accused, proposing that the family bear only half of his fees, payable in installments. Despite his Islamic background, Babiker demonstrated a profound reverence for justice and disdain for oppression, contrasting sharply with the conduct of many of his colleagues in the Islamic movement. He presented a powerful argument aimed at dismissing the charges. Meanwhile, First Sergeant Bashir, the lead investigator, insisted that the accused, Joseph John—nicknamed "Yusuf"—was the murderer. His reasoning was based on the fact that Joseph was the only southerner living in Al-Lamab with that nickname "Yusuf". The incident occurred at 7:00 pm, in front of the victim's family home, and the killer had fled westward—the same direction as the street where Joseph resided.

Sergeant Bashir described the accused as displaying criminal characteristics, such as broken teeth and muscular build. Investigators combed the neighbourhood but found no other southerners with the same nickname. Consequently, he recommended convicting Joseph under Article 251 of the *Penal Code* for premeditated murder. The judge summoned witnesses for testimony. The first witness was the victim's younger brother, Nasr Al-Din Ahmed Sharif, a pharmacy student at the University of Khartoum.

Nasr Al-Din took the oath and recounted: "We were returning from the club around 7:00 pm. Upon reaching our home's gate, we saw two men urinating on the wall. When my brother Mohiy Al-Din asked why they were doing so, one of them drew a knife and stabbed him. The other man exclaimed, 'Why did you kill him, Yusuf?' Yusuf replied, 'Just run!' Both fled westward. I called for help, and my father and others came out, but Mohiy Al-Din had already passed away. We took him to the morgue."

He narrated this and broke into tears in the courtroom. The judge ordered him to remain silent, but his sobbing persisted. Frustrated, the judge instructed that he be escorted out of the courtroom.

The second witness was the victim's father, Sheikh Ahmed Sharif, a retired police officer and a leader of Islamic movement in the area. He stated that he was inside the house when he heard the commotion. Upon stepping outside, he found the victim lying lifeless on the ground.

"As a former police officer who has lived in this neighbourhood for thirty years, I can affirm that there is no one called Yusuf among the South Sudanese here except this man, who appeared in the area four years ago. I believe he is the criminal who killed my son."

Lawyer Babiker sought the court's permission to speak, introducing himself as the defence lawyer, a university professor, and an attorney with ten years of experience. He requested the case be dismissed due to a lack of evidence, arguing that merely sharing a nickname with the killer did not implicate Joseph.

"Your Honour, the assumption that the perpetrator resides in the same neighbourhood as the crime scene is flawed. A criminal can travel from afar to commit a crime and flee. Moreover, the lineup identifying Joseph was prejudiced, as it included individuals only from northern Sudan, under the presumption that the killer's southern accent implicated my client. This accusation lacks evidence. Joseph has no criminal record. His broken teeth resulted from an accident while working honourably as a porter, as attested by many merchants. Similarly, his muscular build stems from lifting heavy materials, not criminal activities. Therefore, Your Honour, I plead with you to dismiss this case and release the accused unconditionally."

The judge adjourned the session, scheduling the next hearing for a month later. The court proceedings dragged on. Two days before the final hearing, the city of Kurmuk in Blue Nile fell to the Sudan People's Liberation Army, led by John Garang. Rumours of military reinforcements approaching the

Gezira State and possibly Khartoum spread, fuelling a wave of hostility toward southerners, who were increasingly viewed as a fifth column. The conflict took on a racial undertone, particularly within state institutions.

Joseph John entered the charged atmosphere of the packed courtroom, flanked by his supporters. Simultaneously, the victim's family chanted for retribution, hurling insults at Attorney Babiker, accusing him of collusion and defending criminals.

These accusations ignored the principle that even the guilty are entitled to legal defence (a right enshrined in law). The political climate, however, lent credence to such claims.

The prosecution lawyer resumed. "Your Honour, given the current state of the country, crimes committed by our southern brethren in Khartoum have surged, such as the recent murder of a shopkeeper in Kalakla. This incident could be connected to the ongoing conflict in Blue Nile. The victim's family unanimously demands the death penalty for the accused. I urge the honourable court to impose a death sentence."

Supporters of Joseph, including northern merchants,

protested chanting, "Freedom, freedom for Yusuf! He is not a criminal!"

Attorney Babiker rose to address the court. "Your Honor, this case is devoid of substantial evidence. Any attempt to link it to events in Blue Nile lacks legal foundation. I respectfully request that this honourable court dismiss the case and release the accused immediately."

After a brief recess for deliberations, the judge returned to the courtroom and delivered the verdict. Joseph John, nicknamed "Yusuf", was sentenced to pay blood money of twenty-one thousand pounds. Failure to pay would result in ten years of imprisonment. The verdict left everyone dissatisfied. The victim's family lamented the court's failure to impose the death penalty, while Joseph's family decried the judgment as unjust, arguing that the case had been politicised. They believed Joseph should have been released immediately due to the lack of evidence implicating him in the crime.

5.

Before the specified date passed, the prosecution filed an appeal before the Supreme Court, which took a few days to decide and ultimately upheld the decision of the lower court. Joseph's family attempted to gather the blood money, but it was difficult despite contributions from businesspeople in Sajana Market.

"We need to raise the money," Anthony Queen said, his voice filled with determination. "Joseph's life depends on it."

"But it's such a large amount," Awanthaji replied, worry etched on his face and then asked, "How will we ever manage?"

Despite their best efforts, the family failed to pay the compensation.

The prison administration decided to transfer Joseph to Port Sudan Prison to serve his sentence, as he could not settle the blood money.

In Port Sudan, Joseph felt isolated and requested a transfer to Kober Prison to allow his family to visit him regularly. This plan enabled family members to make routine visits to him in Kober Prison, especially his cousin Anthony Queen and his friend Awanthaji, who, despite significant efforts to secure his release, were unsuccessful.

"I feel so alone here," Joseph confided in a letter to Anthony. "I need to be closer to you all."

Anthony Queen was a student at the University of Juba, college of Social and Economic Studies, while Awanthaji studied commerce at Zagazig University. They alternated visits to the prison and worked hard to collect funds to pay the blood money. However, the family's financial circumstances did not allow this, and the donations were instead used to cover the lawyer's fees, who had agreed to take half of his dues, out of respect for his relationship with a relative of the accused who worked at his house.

In receiving the letter written by Joseph demanding his transfer back to Kober, Anthony Queen contacted lawyer Babaker who filed the application to the prison administration to transfer Joseph to the Kober Prison and the request was accepted.

After his transfer to Kober Prison, Joseph found an environment conducive to respectful treatment, perhaps due to Kober's political significance within the national capital. The prison hosted political detainees and received frequent visits from foreign delegations, human rights organisations, and diplomatic missions monitoring the situation in Sudan during the era of the Third Democratic Government. This government was composed of the Umma Party and the Democratic Unionist Party, led by Sadiq Al-Sadiq Abdul Rahman Al-Mahdi and Mohammed Osman Ali Al-Mirghani, respectively.

At that time, the National Islamic Front, led by Hassan Abdullah Al-Turabi, occupied the opposition benches in parliament, with Ali Osman Mohammed Taha as leader of the parliamentary opposition. There was also limited representation from southern Sudan political parties since elections were partially conducted in the south due to the ongoing conflict there. Despite Al-Mahdi's stance on the war in the South and his constant efforts to thwart political initiatives aimed at ending the conflict, parliamentary politics followed democratic principles governed by the interests of political parties and organisations, creating a balanced political environment. For instance, the National Islamic Front moved from the opposition to government, while the Democratic Unionist Party exited the government due to its signing of the Mirghani-Garang Agreement in Kokdam, Ethiopia. This anti-peace coalition lasted a year, during which the country's conditions deteriorated and several cities fell into the hands of the Sudan People's Liberation Army fighters. This prompted Prime Minister Sadiq Al-Mahdi to change his position and accept the Mirghani-Garang initiative, leading to the National Islamic Front returning to the opposition benches. Subsequently, an alliance government was re-formed between Al-Mahdi and Al-Mirghani, angering the Islamists, who executed their infamous coup led by Brigadier Omar Hassan Ahmed Al-Bashir, then commander of the military garrison at Mayom in the Western Nuer on June 30, 1989.

Chapter Two

6.

The erosion of justice in Sudan didn't start with Al-Bashir's era. Early signs were already visible during Sadiq Al-Mahdi's tenure, especially with the civil war tearing the country apart.

This was most evident in the south, east, Darfur, the Nuba Mountains, and Blue Nile regions.

On the morning of Friday, June 30, 1989, unusual movements began inside Kober Prison. Significant figures in

Sudanese politics were being brought in for detention. The prison administration requested that some cells be vacated for the new detainees. Those accused of murder, whose sentences were nearing completion, including Joseph John who was transferred to Cell No 9, were all relocated.

The next day, Hassan Al-Turabi and Sadiq Al-Mahdi arrived at Kober Prison. Rumour had it that Al-Turabi's detention was a staged act by the Islamists to conceal their involvement in the military coup. Numerous ministers, parliamentarians, and military generals were also detained.

The situation inside the prison worsened day by day. Joseph received updates about the coup and the country's situation from Sergeant Osman Khater Adam.

A year after seizing power, the National Salvation Government declared jihad in South Sudan, with intensified activities in Kordofan and Darfur, particularly the Nuba Mountains. Training camps for jihadists were established in Kadugli, Laqawa, Al-Muglad, and Al-Dain, most of these centres were established during Sadiq Al-Mahdi's tenure. These camps were supplied with international experts, particularly from countries within the axis of political Islam and

Arab nationalism. This strategy aligned with the National Salvation Government's decision to open Sudan to global Islamic movements while isolating the West. A comprehensive conference held in Khartoum, attended by influential Islamic leaders such as Osama Bin Laden, Ayman Al-Zawahiri, and others, issued resolutions advocating jihad and violence.

Sudan also became a refuge for international fugitives, including Ilich Ramírez Sánchez, famously known as Carlos. He hid in Khartoum until his arrest and extradition to French authorities before the split between Al-Bashir and Al-Turabi.

Islamic groups invested in Sudan, particularly the Taliban and Hamas, channelling funds into infrastructure, agriculture, iron industries, and food production. Projects like the Northern Artery Road, Western Salvation Road, and the Sundus Agricultural Company south of Khartoum were examples of such investments. This plan succeeded, and Sudan experienced significant developmental growth, entering industries such as military manufacturing, pharmaceuticals, vehicles, aircraft, and light and heavy weaponry, particularly in places like Yarmouk, Giad, Kober, and Kereri.

Sudan managed to extract oil with assistance from China,

Malaysia, India, and local militias in the south. Oil exports improved the government's combat capabilities against the Sudan People's Liberation Army.

The Islamists exerted considerable effort to end the war in South Sudan militarily, a strategy planned even before their coup against the constitutional government in Khartoum. Their goal was to resolve the rebellion through military means, resorting to secession only if necessary. This decision to allow the South to separate was ultimately implemented after 22 years of their governance.

The regime attempted to alter the demographics of South Sudan by displacing indigenous populations to exploit resources, especially in Upper Nile and Bahr el Ghazal. This policy aimed to empty the land of its inhabitants, leading to increased attacks by militias, Popular Defence Forces, and jihadists on Southern Sudanese. Media access was restricted to prevent the exposure of the real situation on the ground. However, the split between Al-Turabi and Al-Bashir at the end of 1999 exposed their hidden agenda.

Domestically, the regime implemented its "civilisation project", aiming to change public behaviour and appearance, emphasise Arab identity, and suppress African heritage. Southern Sudanese who migrated northward or to government-controlled areas suffered the most, frequently detained or prosecuted for trivial offenses such as brewing alcohol, improper dress, or alleged collaboration with rebels.

Churches and clubs not reflecting Arab and Islamic culture were also targeted. Public order police and courts were established to monitor and prosecute Southerners, filling prisons with their detainees.

Amid this climate, the war intensified in the south, east, Nuba Mountains, and Ingessana. The Sudan People's Liberation Army took the war to government-controlled areas. The level of public mobilisation by the government exceeded expectations to prevent the capturing of its military garrisons. New recruits were trained and sent to battle zones, and the government invited international allies to visit training camps as a morale boost for jihadists on the front lines.

7.

The Governor of Kordofan received a brief and classified "highly confidential" radio message: "A high-level delegation will arrive. Security arrangements must be prepared to ensure their safety during the mission." The message ended.

The Governor summoned the commander of the Al-Obied military garrison, known as "The Hijana", to his office. "Handle this matter with utmost confidentiality," he instructed.

"Yes, Sir," the commander replied, taking a copy of the radio message with him. Back in his office, the commander called the intelligence officer and the head of the administrative company responsible for VIP protection to brief them on the mission.

The head of the administrative company issued orders to urgently prepare the force, despite the ambiguity of the message. It didn't clarify the identity of the delegation, the timing of their arrival in Al-Obied, the nature of their mission, or their destination. All these questions remained unanswered.

A unit, led by a first sergeant, was assembled and equipped with the necessary tools for the mission. Since the exact timing of the mission's departure had not yet been determined, the first sergeant decided to release the protection company until further notice, instructing them to be ready to regroup when the details of the trip were available.

The personnel dispersed to their homes. The delegation arrived in Al-Obied on a private aircraft around 6:00 pm and headed directly to the government guesthouse. They decided to travel to Kadugli by road at 3:00 am the following morning, Saturday.

The commander of the Al-Obied military garrison instructed the head of the administrative company to send the security team to the delegation's accommodation at the guesthouse to prepare for their early departure. However, the head of the administrative company struggled to regroup the prepared force because some members were unavailable, particularly the first sergeant who was nominated to lead the group. The only solution was to find replacements, including a new team leader. The choice fell on Sergeant Santo. Since it was late on Friday night, the head of the administrative company and the intelligence officer decided to visit Sergeant Santo's home to assign him the task.

"Peace be upon you," the head of administration greeted.

"And peace be upon you," Santo's wife replied.

"Is Santo around?"

"Yes, Sir, I'm here. Is everything alright?" Santo responded, sensing the urgency.

"Sorry to come at this late hour," the head of administration said. "We've got an urgent mission and need you to lead the protection team. The team is already at the guesthouse. Can you get ready and head over there? We don't have anyone else for the task."

"Yes, Sir. Give me two minutes to prepare, and I'll be on my way."

"Thank you. You'll receive final instructions from the delegation at the guesthouse."

Santo packed his bag and headed to the delegation's residence. At the guesthouse, he found the team waiting, including two senior officers from military intelligence, the Popular Defence Forces, and the western sector at the General Command in Khartoum.

Upon arrival Santo first inspected the protection force and proceeded to the Commander of the Popular Defence Forces, Western Sector.

" Sir, the protection force is ready for the mission at dawn; any instructions?" he asked.

"Stay ready as per the schedule. Gather the team at 3:00 am for the trip. Understood?" the commander of the Popular Defence Forces instructed.

"Yes, Sir." Santo saluted

Santo returned to the team and passed on the orders. "You're allowed to dispatch. If anyone needs to go home to fetch something, do it quickly and return. Clear?"

"Clear," the force replied.

At exactly 3:00 am, the force assembled. The Popular Defence Forces' Western Sector Commander arrived and delivered instructions for the journey without revealing the destination.

"You will accompany important figures. Sergeant Santo will travel in the vehicle with the guest, and the rest will be distributed among the other vehicles. Understood?"

"Yes, Sir," the soldiers replied.

The guests boarded their vehicles, and the convoy set off toward Kadugli. Sergeant Santo did not know the identity of the guests. The man in his vehicle bore the demeanour of a religious figure, speaking little but frequently murmuring prayers. About an hour after departing Al Obied, the convoy stopped for dawn prayers. Everyone exited their vehicles except Sergeant Santo. When the western sector commander returned, he found Santo standing by the vehicle, waiting for the guests to board.

"Why didn't you join the prayers?" the commander asked.

"Because I'm a Christian, Sir."

"You're what?"

"A Christian, Sir."

"Then what brought you here?"

"The army, Sir."

The sector commander left Santo standing and boarded his vehicle. Santo followed suit, and the convoy resumed its journey.

Upon reaching Kadugli, the convoy arrived at a hall prepared for a meeting with local security authorities. Sergeant Santo distributed the security personnel and decided to stand at the entrance himself. However, the western sector commander of the Popular Defence Forces ordered him to go and ask the drivers to prepare the vehicles for the return trip.

When Santo went to carry out the orders, he was barred from re-entering the hall, possibly to prevent him from attending the meeting and listening to the agenda of the Islamic delegation's mission to Kadugli.

After the meeting, the delegation visited training camps but did not address the recruits beyond introducing themselves. It was only then that Sergeant Santo learned the names and identities of the guests, including Sheikh Osama Bin Laden, Ayman Al-Zawahiri, and another individual he did not recognise. They were accompanied by the General Command's intelligence director and the Western Sector commander of the Popular Defence Forces.

The delegation returned to Al-Obied and headed straight to the airport to depart for Khartoum. Unfortunately, they arrived late and missed their flight. The delegation decided to return to the guesthouse to spend the night and depart early the following morning.

8.

On the same evening the delegation returned to Al-Obied on their way to Khartoum, Sergeant Santo arrived home at exactly 8:00 pm. Around 9:00 pm, a heavily-armed force appeared and took Santo to the military base, where he found the Garrison Commander waiting for him in his office.

"What's your name?" the Commander asked.

"Sergeant Santo, Sir."

"Where are the guests' documents?"

"Which documents, Sir?"

"You don't know?"

"No, Sir. I don't know anything about the documents."

"You'll know soon," he said in a threatening tone. "Take him to Crocodile," he instructed the intelligence officer.

Santo was handed over to a notorious executioner nicknamed "The Crocodile", who was infamous for executing suspects accused of treason, usually by breaking their necks.

Fortunately for Santo, The Crocodile was bedridden at home with malaria.

Santo spent the night in the military prison, designated for executions, awaiting The Crocodile's return to carry out the task. However, fate had other plans, and Santo's time had not yet come. Meanwhile, in Khartoum, the western sector commander repeatedly contacted the Hajjana Intelligence Unit to ensure Santo's execution was carried out promptly to prevent information about the Islamic delegation's visit to the Popular Defence Forces' training camps from spreading to external circles.

Unaware of The Crocodile's absence, the intelligence commander in Al-Obied assured the Western Sector Commander that strict orders had been issued by the Division Commander to execute Santo and that the matter was settled, with the suspect handed over to the relevant authorities.

On Sunday morning, the Commander was surprised to learn that the orders had not been carried out and that The Crocodile was absent. He assigned another officer, Mohammed Adam, to implement the task.

Mohammed Adam visited the prison to receive the suspect's file and carry out the orders. However, the person to be executed was his neighbour in the military barracks, with whom he frequently shared meals and drinks. Their wives were close friends, and so were their children.

He requested the suspect to be brought to the interrogation office. "Ah, Santo, it's you?" Mohammed held his head in disbelief.

"Yes, Mohammed."

"There is no power or strength except with Allah. Tell me, what happened?"

"Honestly, Mohammed, I know nothing. I just went on the mission yesterday and returned, and then a force came to my house, arrested me, and said the commander wanted to see me. When I got to the office, the commander asked me about some documents. I told him I didn't know anything about them, and he said, 'You'll know them,' before ordering my handover to The Crocodile."

For the second time, Mohammed Adam exclaimed, "There is no power or strength except with Allah! Don't worry, bro."

He left the interrogation room at around 10:00 am, and went to Santo's house to reassure his family and explain what had happened. Despite the gravity of the situation, he promised that Santo's case was in safe hands. He also informed his own wife, Zeinab, about Santo's predicament. She cried bitterly, but he comforted her, saying everything would be alright. She thanked him and expressed her fondness for Santo and his family, especially Madam Teresa.

"We hope no harm comes to them," she said.

Mohammed Adam returned to the base at around 3:00 pm and entered the intelligence commander's office to find out more about the fabricated case against Santo and assess its seriousness.

"So, Mohammed, have you carried out the orders?" the intelligence commander asked.

"Not yet, Sir. But what's the issue with this man?"

"Just go and execute the orders, and then ask questions later. The leadership has decided. Is that clear?"

"Understood, Sir."

Mohammed returned to the prison with a box of cigarettes and found Santo still in the same room. He sat down and said, "Santo, you're still here."

"Where would I go, Mohammed?"

"I left you here so you could escape, Santo."

"I can't escape, Mohammed. I'm not guilty."

"Do they know that?" Mohammed offered Santo a cigarette and took one himself. Santo apologized, saying, "I quit smoking, Mohammed."

"Oh, since when?"

"A while ago."

"Good, that's great. Tell me honestly, what's going on?" Mohammed took out a paper and ruled it with a ruler.

Santo recounted everything: how the administrative company's commander and the intelligence officer visited his home late Friday night, asking him to lead the security team for important figures arriving from Khartoum. Since the first person assigned to the mission was unavailable, they asked him to prepare to lead the team. He went to the guesthouse, found the team ready, and they departed at 3:00 am for Kadugli. An hour into the journey, the vehicles stopped for prayers. Everyone got out except him. When the Western Sector Commander of the Popular Defence Forces returned from the prayers and found him standing by the vehicle, he asked why he hadn't joined the prayers.

Santo told him, "I'm a Christian."

The commander was surprised by his response and asked, "Then why are you here?"

Santo replied, "The army brought me, Sir."

The commander turned away and got into his car. When

they arrived in Kadugli, he ordered Santo to leave the meeting hall under the pretext of preparing the vehicles so they could depart quickly after the meeting finished. When they returned to Al-Obied, Santo went home, only to be surprised by a heavily armed military force arresting him and taking him to the Military Headquarters, where he found the Commander waiting for him.

Upon entering, the Commander asked, "What's your name?" When Santo answered, the Commander said, "Where are the documents?"

Santo asked, "Which documents, Sir?"

The Commander said, "You'll know them," and then ordered the soldiers, "Take him and hand him over to The Crocodile. That's the whole story in brief."

"Alright, thank you. I understand now why they want to kill you. You knew their jihadist plan, and they think you'll reveal this secret to others. They intended to kill you on Saturday night after their return, but The Crocodile was sick. Don't worry; I'll make sure you're safe. I've been ordered to execute you, but I won't do it."

Mohammed Adam continued, "You know, Santo? Despite

my anger towards Southerners because of Brig. Dominic's actions against me since he stripped me of my rank from First Sergeant to Private and dismissed me from the army in the Equatoria Military Garrison five years ago, I still hold great respect for you and your family. If you had been a Fertit (like Brig. Dominic), I wouldn't have helped you, but since you're a Dinka, I'll support you until the end. The Dinka are men of honour, and as a Riziegi, I admire warriors. I despise cowards. I gave you the chance to escape, but you didn't take it. If you were a Fertit, you would have run away." He patted Santo on the back, visibly upset with Brig. Dominic.

Mohammed Adam left the interrogation room at around 5:00 pm and went to the intelligence office with the report in hand.

"What's up?" the intelligence commander asked.

"It's done, Sir. Here's the report."

"What report, man?"

"The investigation."

"Who asked you for an investigation?"

"But, Sir, there's no justification for executing this man. He's innocent. Moreover, the information has already leaked, and killing him now would cause a bigger problem since

Brig. Robert knows about it and won't stay silent."

"Did this information reach Brig. Robert?"

"Yes, Sir, he knows."

"What's the solution then? The Commander wanted him dead."

"There's no way, Sir. He will cause trouble in the Military Garrison."

"So what shall we do now?"

"He has to be released."

"Fine, let's look at this tomorrow."

After leaving the Intelligence Commander's office, Mohammed Adam went to Brig. Robert's residence to explain the situation. Brig. Robert is the second in command in the Military Garrison.

Mohammed saluted Brig. Robert and said, "Sir, those people wanted to kill that man. You have to intervene tomorrow with the Commander."

"Who?" Brig. Robert asked in shock.

"You don't know Santo is detained, and the Commander wants him dead, Sir?"

"How is that possible?"

"I swear by God, it's true. We'll tell you everything later, but make sure he's released today. It is between me and you, Sir."

"Thank you very much, Mohammed."

- - -

The next morning, after the assembly, Brig. Robert entered the commander's office in the presence of the intelligence officer and asked, "Sir, hand over Sergeant Santo's body; his family wanted it for burial."

"What body, Brig. Robert?"

"The soldier you sent to Kadugli and murdered."

The Commander turned to the intelligence commander, "Did you hear what Brig.

Robert said?"

"Yes, Sir," the intelligence officer responded.

"Can you bring this soldier and hand him over to him?"

"Yes, Sir."

The intelligence officer fetched Sergeant Santo and handed him over to Brig. Robert, releasing him without conditions before The Crocodile could recover and return to duty to receive the prison management from Mohammed Adam.

Santo got out, but it was merely the starting point of crises that would pursue the man in his favourite battalion, the Fifth Infantry, known as the Hajjana.

- - -

The following day, the Commander summoned the intelligence officer to his office.

"Salute, sir."

"Sit down."

"What's going on, exactly? How did this man escape?"

"This is strange, sir. I'm quite astonished, myself. You know, after you instructed me to hand him over to The Crocodile, the soldiers went and found The Crocodile ill, and they didn't act or even return to inform me of what had happened. So the man stayed asleep in detention. When I learned of this, I called Mohammed Adam to execute the orders, but he brought me a lengthy report, twenty-eight pages long. I told him we didn't want the report; but he said nothing could be done to eliminate this man because Brig. Robert's men were already aware of the information. And indeed, that was the situation the following day after the assembly."

"Okay, the important thing is that this matter is settled, but this man poses a threat to the army."

"I know, sir. Let's see what we can do about him," the intelligence officer replied.

9.

After Santo's release, he felt targeted because of his faith. Everything that happened to him could have led to his death were it not for divine intervention that left The Crocodile bedridden, saving his life that fateful night. Since the army leadership had decided to eliminate him, it was only a matter of time before the plan was executed.

Santo discussed the matter with his wife, Teresa, who advised him to consult with Mohammed Adam, who had made great efforts to save his life. Santo then went to Mohammed Adam's house.

Mohammed Adam's wife, Zeinab, who had played a behind-the-scenes role, was overjoyed to see Santo for the first time since his release. "Praise be to God for your safety, Santo," Zeinab said.

"Thank you, Zeinab. You played a significant role in my release. Teresa told me about it," Santo replied.

"It was our duty. You're a good man, Santo. Let God spare you from harm."

"Thank you, Zeinab. You did the best. Where's my brother Mohammed?"

"He just stepped out."

"Alright, I just came to thank you for saving my life. Honestly, if not for you and your husband Mohammed, I would be among the dead now."

"God forbid! Don't say that, Santo. You're a good man, and your children need you the most."

"Thank you, Zeinab. Please let Mohammed know I came when he returns home."

At 7:00 pm, Mohammed arrived at Santo's house.

"Greetings, my dear Santo. I'm glad to see you back with your family. Zeinab told me you visited us?"

"Yes, Mohammed, I went to thank you for what you did. My family and I will never forget this favour."

"Santo, it wasn't your time to die. What saved you was The Crocodile's illness. After your release, he came asking, 'Where's that rat, Mohammed? He hates you intensely.' I told him you were released. He said, 'That son of a dog! If I'd found him here today, I would've squeezed the life out of him, even if he were Robert's own son.'"

"But why does he hate me, Mohammed?" Santo asked.

"There's no reason, really. The man is addicted to taking lives. You know he has killed many people here."

"May God forgive him," Santo sympathetically responded

Teresa brought them dinner. "Please, have some dinner," she said.

"Thank you, Teresa. I came home then straight away to your house." Mohammed appreciated the dinner.

Washing his hands, Santo said, "You know, Mohammed, I came to consult you on something."

"What is it, Santo? Tell me."

"I want to resign from the army."

"Come on, there is no way. They won't allow it. They'll

use it as an excuse to frame you for something and get rid of you, especially after what happened in Kadugli."

"You're right, Mohammed. But what's the solution? I'm feeling terrible here with the Hajjana and don't want to continue."

"Let me suggest something to you."

"What do you suggest then?"

"Apply for a leave. Take a break and maybe travel outside Al-Obied for a while, Santo."

"That's a good idea, Mohammed."

"Thank you, Santo. Good night."

"Good night, Mohammed."

- - -

The next morning, Santo went to Brig. Robert's office to thank him for his role in his release. "Good morning, sir." He saluted.

"Good morning. Please, have a seat. Are you fine, Sergeant Santo?"

"Yes, sir. Thank God." Santo began speaking in Dinka language, "I came to thank you for saving my life."

"You have nine lives, Santo! Were it not for divine will, you'd have left this world.

But the Lord has his plans; no one dies before their time."

"I'm feeling stressed and would like to request leave to rest a bit. I'm thinking of going to Wau to visit the family there."

"That sounds good, Santo. Go ahead and submit the request."

Santo stood, saluted, and said, "Thank you, Sir."

He left Brig. Robert's office, took the leave, and travelled to Wau. After his leave ended, he faced difficulties flying back to Al-Obied and decided to join Wau military garrison in Greenti, where he remained stationed for over a year while regularly visiting the military headquarters.

The intelligence unit in Al-Obied reported to its headquarters in Khartoum about Sergeant Santo's defection after taking leave and travelling to Wau. The Intelligence Directorate sent a very short message to Wau military garrison, inquiring about Sergeant Santo's whereabouts. The message read;

Sergeant Santo of the Hajjana's music corps, is to be located and reported back. End.

The Wau Garrison responded with the message:

Sergeant Santo is here in Wau. He intends to return to Al-Obied by the first available flight.

10.

Santo returned from Wau to find his family's situation deteriorated. Everyone in the neighbourhood, except Mohammed's family and his wife Zeinab, who knew the truth, looked at them as outcasts and traitors. They were accused of providing intelligence to the rebellion about the movements of the armed forces, the Popular Defence Forces, and the Mujahideen, particularly at the Nuba Mountains front. The family lived in complete isolation after rumours spread that Santo had joined the rebellion in Wau.

In the morning, Santo went to the administration, only to find that everything had changed; even his closest friends had distanced themselves. His friend Mohammed Adam explained everything to him, including the leadership's attempts to implicate him and throw him back into prison. He warned that The Crocodile was waiting for such an opportunity to execute his revenge. Mohammed advised Santo to leave the Hajjana immediately if possible.

"You were right when you said you wanted to leave the army," Mohammed said.

"You're right, Mohammed. I agree. Even my children are uncomfortable at home and don't want to stay here. The Hajjana is no longer the unit we once knew, where people of different backgrounds worked together. The Islamists have ruined it, turning it into a place of ethnic discrimination and racism. But how do I get out of this mess, my brother?"

"Go and talk to the intelligence officer about this. The last time rumours about your defection surfaced, I went to him, and he said that Santo hadn't defected. But the Commander dislikes you and wants to get rid of you by any means," Mohammed revealed.

"Alright, let's go and see him," Santo agreed.

- - -

"Greetings, sir!" Santo saluted the intelligence officer.

"And greetings to you, the great rebel," the intelligence officer replied sarcastically.

"I returned yesterday from Wau after a long absence and thought I should come and greet you."

"Thank God for your safety, Santo. They said you'd defected," he smiled.

"Seriously, sir?" Santo asked.

"Have you not heard the news, Santo?"

"Not at all, Sir. But I found my colleagues distant from me, and even my family felt a significant change in the neighbourhood," Santo replied in a polite way, hiding the fact that he had heard the news about his defection. Santo continued, "Sir, I've come to speak with you about this matter frankly. I am innocent and deeply love the Hajjana. It has become like my home, and the people here are like my family. But recently, I've felt there's a plan to eliminate me, especially since the visit of the Islamic delegation led by Bin Laden. That's why I'm asking for your help."

"What do you want me to do for you, Santo?"

"Just help me transfer to the Kosti military garrison."

"That's not possible with the current commander. But let's think about it if he's transferred to another division. It won't be Kosti either," he smiled.

Not long after, a message came announcing that the Military Garrison Commander would be transferred to the General Command in Khartoum next month. The intelligence officer mentioned this to Santo, advising him to wait patiently until the current Commander leaves and the new one takes over.

- - -

A month later, the intelligence officer summoned Sergeant Santo to his office.

"Greetings, sir," Santo said.

"The man could leave at any moment from now. Go and prepare your transfer request to the new commander and submit it as soon as he takes over."

"Yes, sir," Santo replied. He saluted and left.

Santo wrote the transfer request to move from Al-Obied to Kosti. The new commander approved it immediately.

Santo left the Al-Obied military garrison with his family and settled in Kosti, where he remained until he retired from the army. However, the memories of Bin Laden's and Ayman Al-Zawahiri's debacle never left him.

Chapter Three

11.

Following the Global Islamic Conference in Khartoum, the state adopted new policies under the slogan "The Civilisational Project", which called for a return to the roots and traditions of the early Islamic state. The West, Christianity, and Southern Sudanese were labelled as the most dangerous enemies of Islam. Relations with America and many European countries were identified and associated with this axis. The United States was designated as the primary enemy—

second only to Israel, which Sudan had boycotted since the "Three No's Summit" in Khartoum (No peace, no recognition, no negotiation with the Zionist enemy).

Jihadist songs emerged to boost the morale of fighters, such as the anthem "I am a Muslim" by Sheikh Yusuf al-Qaradawi, which proclaimed:

> *My constitution and my path are the Book of God.*
> *The guide of my journey is Muhammad,*
> *the Messenger of God.*

> *My homeland is wherever God's call resonates.*
> *My people are the nation of Islam; they are my party*
> *and the party of God.*

Another song went like this:

> *Oh Americans, we trained for you.*
> *Our country is not Panama,*
> *And our president is not Noriega.*

(It refers to the U.S. war against Panama and the arrest of its former president Manuel Noriega).

During this critical phase in Sudan's history, filled with fervour and an intense disregard for non-Arab and non-Islamic ethnic and religious groups, presidential decrees were issued to regulate society, alter the social landscape, and enforce Islamic dress codes, particularly the hijab for women in state institutions, universities, and schools. Mandatory military training was imposed on all government employees, especially senior civil servants. Prayer was made compulsory in workplaces, with institutions required to build mosques on their premises and monitor those who did not pray, subjecting them to retirement. These measures had a profound impact on the army and organised forces.

Churches faced restrictions on obtaining permits, monitoring of their activities, and confiscation of their properties—most notably the Catholic Church premises on Airport Road, which was converted into the headquarters of the National Congress Party due to its strategic location. The justification was that having a church at such a strategic location where foreign visitors pass contradicted the notion of an Islamic state in Sudan. This same ideology nearly cost Sergeant Santo his life during Osama Bin Laden and Ayman al-Zawahiri's visit to the Mujahideen camps in Kadugli.

The judiciary was one of the institutions most affected by these changes, with senior judges forced into retirement and loyalists to the regime appointed in their positions. The judicial system was reviewed, and past cases were revisited to incriminate opponents, imprison them, or eliminate them.

The situation in Southern Sudan, Nuba Mountains, and Blue Nile regions deteriorated further. Mujahideen forces were mobilised to suppress rebellions, displace civilians, and extend a program initiated by former Prime Minister Sadiq Al-Mahdi. A horrifying development occurred in Ed Daein, South Darfur, where innocent Southern citizens were burned alive in a train carriage. Moreover, the region witnessed attacks by Murahaleen militias involving the abduction of thousands of women and children, many of whom remain in Kordofan and Darfur to this day.

In Equatoria, a destructive war unfolded with jihadist battalions beginning with students who were forced to fight as part of mandatory military service before being allowed to enrol in universities. These Mujahideen often retaliated against civilians when defeated by the Sudan People's Liberation Army (SPLA), as seen in Juba and other areas. Oil fields in Southern Sudan were exploited to fuel the war against its people, with local militias trained and armed to destabilise the region.

Southern Sudanese returning from abroad were targeted, monitored, and arrested upon their return for fabricated accusations. For instance, Anthony Queen, a cousin of Joseph John Bak, was arrested in Wadi Halfa upon returning from Egypt because Egyptian authorities had shown leniency in travel procedures at Aswan port. At that time, Egypt had tightened checks on passengers travelling to Sudan due to Sudan's open-door policy for Islamic groups.

When it was Queen's turn at Aswan port, an Egyptian officer took his passport and greeted him warmly: "Anthony Queen, come aboard. You are welcomed. Where's your luggage?"

Queen boarded the ferry without being searched like other Sudanese passengers. This did not sit well with Sudanese security personnel on the same ferry.

Upon arrival in Wadi Halfa: "Where is that rascal called Anthony Queen?" a Sudanese officer demanded. Silence enveloped the place. Since Queen was the only Southern Sudanese on board: "Aren't you Anthony Queen?" asked the officer.

"Yes," Queen replied.

"Why are you quiet? Stand up. Where's your luggage?"

"Here's my luggage," Queen responded.

"Come with me."

Queen was arrested for three days without any charges simply because Egyptian authorities hadn't searched him. This was reality for Southern Sudanese in their own country.

In Kalakla too, seven members of one family were executed on false charges of murdering a shop owner—an accusation motivated solely by their Southern Sudanese ethnicity.

These factors led Southerners to overwhelmingly vote for independence in a referendum resulting in establishment of the Republic of South Sudan in 2011.

12.

The judiciary, public prosecutions, police, and the entire justice system were affected by the new revolutionary policies, resulting in the dismissal of judges and legal councillors and the appointment of others loyal to the regime in their places. Additionally, the regular forces, including the police, prisons, game wardens, and firefighters, were merged into a single force called the "Unified Police". This system allowed officers to transfer between various units without restriction, facilitating the dismissal of non-loyal elements and their replacement with loyalists. Most judges were dismissed, and regime loyalists were appointed to courts and prison administration.

Lieutenant Colonel Yassin, the cousin of the late Mohiy Al-Din, was appointed as the officer in charge of cells and political detainees in Kober Prison. These changes also extended to other institutions.

After Yassin took charge of the prison, the conditions for the detainee Joseph John worsened significantly. Visits to him were restricted unless allowed by Yassin personally.

Joseph could no longer receive information from outside as he once had, and any prison officers interacting with him faced dismissal.

No one inside the prison knew of the family connection between the late Mohiy Al-Din and Lieutenant Colonel Yassin until after Joseph's execution. Yassin used his political and Islamic background to organise a visit by Sheikh Osama Bin Laden to the prison, with the intention of allowing him to meet with prisoners and demand confessions for their alleged crimes, promising to pay fines or compensation for those unable to pay, but only after exerting pressure.

Indeed, Bin Laden visited Kober Prison, in what was portrayed as a charitable act, at least according to his personal interpretation. Nevertheless, it turned into a disaster for Joseph John, who thought it was a golden opportunity to secure his release. He was unaware of the conspiracy Lieutenant Colonel Yassin had orchestrated against him. Joseph made this decision without consulting anyone, perhaps due to the absence of his cousin Anthony Queen, who was abroad, or his friend Awantaji, who was in Egypt pursuing his studies. Joseph, along with other prisoners, submitted their requests through the prison administration, including a certificate of his conversion to Islam, despite being a Catholic Christian.

Lieutenant Colonel Yassin, instead of forwarding Joseph's request to Bin Laden's office, saw it as an opportunity for revenge against the man he blamed for his cousin's death. He immediately went to his uncle, Ahmed Sharif, at his house in Al-Imbab, White Nile, at five in the evening. He knocked on the door forcefully and with excitement.

Sheikh Ahmed, surprised, asked, "Who's there?"

"It's me, Yassin, Uncle."

He opened the door. "Come in, Yassin. How are you doing?"

"I'm fine, Uncle. Finally, the criminal has confessed."

"What do you mean?"

"By God Almighty," Yassin said, handing him the document. "Here's his confession."

"Finally! Praise be to God. So, what do we do now?" Sheikh Ahmed asked.

"Let's sit in the living room, and I'll explain everything, Uncle."

"Alright, come in, my son."

DR DHIEU MATHOK DIING WOL

"You know, Uncle, we need to reopen the case and use this confession. The reason the death penalty wasn't issued earlier was the lack of evidence. Now we have the evidence in our hands, and we must go to the lawyer to start the procedures immediately."

"That's a great idea, Yassin. But can a case that was ruled six years ago be reopened?"

"That's what we need to work on, Uncle. There have been major changes in the judicial system, and we must take advantage of having our people in the judiciary."

"You're right, Yassin. Let's go to Lawyer Abdel Azim."

They left for Abdel Azim's residence in Khartoum Two. Arriving at the lawyer's house, Yassin knocked on the door, and the guard informed them that the lawyer was out of the country and would return in a week.

"Thank you. No problem," Yassin said as they got into the car.

"What do we do now?" Sheikh Ahmed asked.

"We'll have to wait for him, Uncle."

"Alright, that's fine. It will all work out with God's blessings."

Sheikh Ahmed returned to his house, while Yassin continued his journey to Al-Sahafa, where his family lived.

13.

Before proceeding to court, the Secretary of the Islamic Movement in Khartoum State wrote a letter to the judge of the Criminal Court in Al-Shajara, the court of jurisdiction, requesting a reconsideration of the case. His letter read:

To His Honor, Judge Sharaf Al-Din Fadl Al-Mola,
Peace, mercy, and blessings of Allah be upon you,
I pray this letter finds you in good health.

I wish to draw your attention to case number 43/1986, in which Joseph John Bak, known as "Yusuf", is accused of murdering Mohiy Al-Din Ahmed Sharif. This is a matter of integrity, where the blood of a Muslim was shed in cold blood. We must restore dignity to the family. The lawyer, Mr. Abdel Azim Farouk, will present new evidence, including the killer's confessions. Although this case was adjudicated six years ago, it must be reviewed,

and the victim's family should be given the opportunity

to appeal and reconsider the verdict due to the emergence

of new evidence.

May Allah bless and reward you abundantly.
Your brother,

Ezzedine Abdelkader Al-Mujtaba
Secretary of the Islamic Movement in Khartoum State

Before Lawyer Abdel Azim could submit the documents for appeal supported by the written and fingerprinted confessions of the accused, Joseph John, Sheikh Ahmed Sharif, the father of the late Mohiy Al-Din, visited the judge at his home and handed him the letter from the Secretary of the Islamic Movement in Khartoum State.

The following day, the case was appealed to the higher court, and a new panel was formed to review it. Within three weeks, the Appeal Court issued a decision to reopen the case and revise the penalty, sentencing the accused to death.

The court scheduled an urgent session to notify the accused and the victim's family of the higher court's decision without hearing from the defendant or witnesses. Joseph was brought to the session alone, without his lawyer or family, under the impression that it was a session to announce his release following the charitable initiative by Sheikh Osama Bin Laden. However, it turned out to be a session to declare a new decision by the higher court. The previous verdict, which had required Joseph to pay blood money amounting to twenty-one thousand Sudanese pounds or serve ten years in prison if unpaid, was replaced with a new verdict; execution by hanging until death.

Sergeant Osman, who escorted the defendant, proclaimed:

"It was truly a sad day in the history of our country and for the prisoner Joseph John who had already served more than half his sentence. It was a day that confirmed the destruction of the justice system by the Islamists. This incident must not go unchallenged.

This marks the absence of justice and the collapse of the judicial system in the country."

14.

The court's decision was shocking not only to Joseph but also to all the prisoners and wardens at Kober Prison, including the political detainees, who expressed their concern about the state of the country under Islamists' rule. This decision symbolised the collapse and erosion of the principles of justice in the country.

Sergeant Osman, who had accompanied Joseph to court, returned to the prison deeply disheartened. He went to Colonel Muawiya Ma'moun, the Deputy Director of the Prison and requested a two-day leave to rest.

"Good morning, Sir."

"Good morning, Osman."

"Did you hear what happened yesterday with the prisoner Joseph?"

"Yes, I heard he went back to court for a settlement after Osama Bin Laden paid the blood money for him."

"Not at all! He was taken back to court to have his previous sentence reconsidered."

"What? How is that possible?"

"I swear, Sir, it's true."

"But how can a case that's been closed for six years be reopened, especially when he only has four years left to complete his sentence?"

"Sir, these are the Islamists. Nothing is impossible for them."

"What about the legal principle of double jeopardy, which prevents a person from being tried twice for the same crime?"

"What do you mean, Sir?"

"That principle ensures that a person cannot be sentenced twice for the same case, as it undermines justice."

"Well, Sir, they just sentenced him again."

"That can only happen under one condition."

"What condition is that, Sir?"

"If new evidence is found that wasn't available at the time of the original verdict."

"Oh, so that's why…"

"Why what, Osman?"

"They tricked Joseph into making confessions through Bin Laden and then submitted the document to the court.

"What are you talking about, Osman?"

"It's unethical and inhumane, Sir."

"You're absolutely right, Osman. Look at what they've done to the prison administration—bringing in people from nowhere to lead an institution that's been around for over a hundred years."

"Sir, do you know that Lieutenant Colonel Yassin turned out to be a relative of the late Mohiy Al-Din, the man Joseph is accused of killing? He's actually his cousin."

"Unbelievable!"

"Yes, that's why he pushed so hard to overturn the original court ruling and enforce the death sentence. Poor Joseph…"

"It's not just about Joseph, Osman. The entire country is in turmoil, I swear."

"May God help us all, Sir. By the way, there's something else I need to discuss with you, Sir."

"What is it, Osman?"

"Joseph asked me to bring him a priest to pray for him."

"That's a good idea, especially after the Bin Laden incident. But how will that work inside the prison?"

"That's the problem, Sir. The Islamists won't allow a priest to enter the prison for prayers."

"Then I'll take Joseph's request and go to Comboni Al-Majaneen to look for a priest."

"Comboni Al-Majaneen?"

"Yes, Sir," he laughed. "That's where most Southerners gather, especially on Fridays and Sundays, for free education. That's why it's called Comboni Majaneen (Free of charges' Comboni)."

"Alright, I'll grant you a three-day leave to find the priest and arrange prayers for him before the execution."

"Thank you, Sir."

Colonel Muawiya Ma'moun was a member of the African National Front (ANF) at the University of Khartoum. After graduating from the Faculty of Law, he joined the prison academy and graduated as a captain, rose in its ranks and became Colonel. He was one of the few officers who advocated for the vision of a "New Sudan", as championed by the late Dr. John Garang de Mabior, the founder of the Sudan People's Liberation Movement/Army (SPLM/A).

15.

Osman arrived at the Comboni Al-Majaneen in central Khartoum near Abu Jinzeer Square on Sunday at 10:00 am. The place was bustling with activities: free private lessons for students, family meetings, prayers, and more, all happening simultaneously.

Unsure of what to do, Osman approached one of the attendees and asked, "Excuse me, I'm sorry to bother you. May I ask you something?"

"Go ahead, sir," the attendee replied.

"I'd like to speak with a priest."

"Alright, let him finish the prayers, and I'll let him speak to you."

"Okay, thank you."

Osman waited for a while, and soon the priest arrived.

"Peace be with you. I am Father Emmanuel Franco. How can I help you?"

"Thank you, Father. I'm Sergeant Osman Khater from Kober Prison."

"Kober Prison?!" The priest looked surprised. "Why are you here?"

"No need to worry, Father. I've come seeking your help."

"Go ahead," the priest replied with a smile, looking more at ease.

"There's a man sentenced to death in the prison, and the execution might happen soon. He asked me to contact a priest to pray for him. He says he lied about being the killer; he's not the murderer."

"Why would he do that?"

"He hoped Bin Laden would pay the blood money for him. They told him he needed to convert to Islam, after which the payment could be made. But unfortunately, it turned out to be a deception by the deceased's relative within the prison administration."

"Now what do you need from me, Osman?"

"I need you to come to the prison and pray for him, if they allow you inside."

"And if they don't? You know those people better than I do."

"You could pray for him in absentia, I believe. Is it possible in Christianity?"

"Yes, it's possible. In Christianity, we pray for freedom and forgiveness for prisoners. I am here to serve God, Osman."

"Alright. I'll return to work on Tuesday. Can you come to Kober Prison at around 1:00 pm in the afternoon?"

"I agree. I'll see you then, God willing. But wait, may I ask you something?"

"Go ahead, Father."

"Are you a Christian?"

"Not at all. I'm Muslim."

"Why are you so concerned about this?"

"Because Joseph is innocent, and all religions, including Islam, stand against injustice."

"I understand. May God be with you always, Osman."

"Thank you, Father. See you, God willing."

16.

On Tuesday at 1:00 pm, Father Emmanuel arrived at the main gate of Kober Prison with another person. Nonetheless, the guards at the gate stopped them and asked them to contact Sergeant Osman Khater for permission to enter, and they did. After some inspection, the guards found that the priest was carrying a Bible, which angered them. They instructed the priest not to bring the Bible inside. The priest insisted on taking the holy book with him, but the guards refused and escalated the matter to Lieutenant Colonel Yassin in the detainees' unit. Yassin ordered not only that the Bible be left at the gate but also that the priest should not be allowed to enter.

The priest agreed to leave but asked the guards for a favour: to call Sergeant Osman Khater again. When Osman arrived, he apologised to the priest and wondered whether they could perform the prayer in absentia.

The priest explained the concept of absentia prayers in Christianity: "It's a prayer for the dead, with or without the presence of the body, as the prayer is for the soul, not the flesh. However, it might be unethical to perform a prayer for someone who is still alive, even if they're heading to the gallows tomorrow. Rest assured, we will pray for Joseph so that God may forgive his sins. This is a prayer we offer for any believer seeking repentance and forgiveness, especially prisoners, the sick, and the oppressed. All these rituals are part of Christian family traditions. I understand Joseph needs prayers and will face death soon. He will remain in my prayers always."

Then, the priest asked for the full name of the accused and the details of his case, advising that Joseph pray and fast. Then, the priest and his companion departed.

On Sunday at the Comboni, Joseph John's name was included in the believers' prayers, which were petitions offered by the congregation for those in need of divine service. The attendees participated in the prayers and offered sacrifices for Joseph, asking God to forgive his sins.

Chapter Four

17.

After a long absence on a three-month trip to the Arab Republic of Egypt, Anthony Queen returned to Sudan on the same journey during which he was arrested by the National Security in Wadi Halfa. This was due to the leniency shown to him by the Egyptian authorities at a time when Sudanese travellers were being subjected to severe beatings and thorough inspections by the same authorities. Consequently, Anthony Queen was beaten and detained for three days in the National Security detention centres in Wadi Halfa as an act of retaliation for the Egyptian security's treatment of Sudanese at the Aswan River Port.

This was not Anthony Queen's first experience with such arrests, as he held a leadership position in the Juba University Southern Sudan Students' Association (JUSSSA). He was previously detained at the Ramila Complex of Juba University along with other southern students who protested against the Arabisation policies in Sudanese universities. This was particularly significant at Juba University, where the medium of instruction was English, but the regime in Khartoum forced both professors and students to adopt Arabic as the language of education, ordering everybody to study the Arabic language. Such incidents were a recurring pattern for southern students in Sudanese universities, especially JUSSSA, ANF, and all southern student organisations in other universities. These actions aimed to implement demographic changes, enforce the civilisation project, and create an Arab Muslim society loyal to Arabism and Islam in Sudan.

Returning to the prison visit, Anthony Queen arrived in Khartoum on Saturday. On Sunday, around eleven o'clock, he visited Kober Prison to meet the prisoner Joseph John, whom he had not seen during his three months in Egypt. To his shock, he discovered that Joseph was no longer in the prison.

At the main entrance designated for visitors' procedures, he greeted a guard:

"Peace be upon you." "Peace be upon you, too."

"I'd like to enter, please."

"Who are you visiting?"

"I'd like to visit the prisoner, Joseph John."

"Joseph John? That man was executed a while ago."

"Executed?"

"Yes, he was executed about a month ago. You didn't know?"

"Not at all. I was out of the country."

"Well, he's gone."

"Can you please call Sergeant Osman Khater for me?" Anthony Queen politely requested.

"Osman left the job."

"Why did he leave?"

"He resigned two weeks ago."

"Do you know where he is now?"

95

"No. But they say he lives in Al-Haj Yusuf, Street One, near the last bus station."

"Thank you."

Anthony Queen then left.

18.

Anthony Queen arrived at the last bus station in Al-Haj Yusuf, Street One, and asked a young man at the station, who informed him that he was Osman's younger brother. The young man then took Anthony to their home.

At home, Osman welcomed Anthony with tears in his eyes, saying, "May God have mercy on him. Come, let's sit here."

He took Anthony's hand and led him to the living room, where his younger brother brought some water for drinking.

Anthony Queen said, "Osman, tell me what really happened."

"You know, after the Islamists came to power, there were significant changes in the prison administration and the judiciary. At Kober Prison, they brought in a man named

Yassin with the rank of lieutenant colonel. He had no military training whatsoever; rather he used to be a teacher in primary schools. Suddenly, he found himself as a lieutenant colonel in the prison system. This man was related to the late Mohiy Al-Din Ahmed Sharif, whom Joseph was accused of killing. Since the moment Yassin entered the prison administration, things began to change for the worse. He imposed strict measures on Joseph and worked day and night to change his sentence to execution. His final attempt was to invite Sheikh Osama Bin Laden to visit the prison, asking the prisoners who were unable to pay blood money to confess their crimes publicly, hoping Bin Laden would cover their dues. This was the trap Joseph fell into because, after Yassin obtained Joseph's confession, he took it to the appeals court. With the court's cooperation, the case and sentence were revisited."

"How could that happen, Osman?" Anthony Queen asked.

"That's exactly what happened. We in the prison administration received the court's invitation for the session and thought it would lead to Joseph's release after Bin Laden paid the blood money. But, to our great shock, it turned out to be a session to reconsider the verdict six years later. This is the collapse of justice under the Islamists in this country."

"So how was the execution carried out? No one in the family was informed?" Queen inquired.

"The day before the execution, I and another officer were asked to accompany Joseph to visit one of his relatives. Joseph asked to go to his uncle, General Morris Tong, in Al-Taif. Unfortunately, we didn't find him at home. We waited there for over an hour until a young man came and said his father wasn't home. We left and returned to the prison. I thought his father might come to the prison after being informed of the visit, but that didn't happen. The next morning at dawn, Joseph was taken to the gallows and executed."

Both Anthony Queen and Osman wept.

"What were his final words?" Queen asked.

"He was deeply saddened by Yassin's deception. He wasn't remorseful about his death because he knew he hadn't committed the murder. But what tormented him was the lie he told, claiming to be the killer, and his conversion to Islam. He wanted to share this story with his uncle so that his mother would know he didn't commit the crime."

"Why didn't he tell his cousin, whom you found at the house?" Queen further asked.

"I don't know. He was deeply upset about the situation and asked me to bring a priest to the prison for repentance and prayers. We tried, but he didn't meet the priest. Fortunately, Father Emmanuel said he would pray for him. Later, I learned that the prayer was held at the Comboni Al-Majaneen. May God accept him."

"So all he wanted was to tell this story?"

"Yes, that's what he said."

"I'll convey his concerns," Anthony Queen concluded. "Let me ask you something."

"Of course," said Osman.

"Why did you leave your job?" asked Anthony.

"I was deeply affected by the injustice that befell this kind man. I knew Joseph wasn't the killer, but the world's injustice took his life. I felt uneasy in the prison, especially when I saw the cell where Joseph served his unfair sentence.

"Secondly, I was being targeted by Lieutenant Colonel Yassin and feared getting into trouble with him because both Colonel Muawiya and I were labelled as anti-Islamist government. Thirdly, my mother is a Dinka by tribe. My father worked in the railway police in Bahr el Ghazal, met my mother, Fatima Nawai, and married her. I see Joseph as a maternal uncle."

"That's remarkable, Osman. I've always felt a connection between you and Joseph but couldn't figure out what it was. I decided to wait and see. Can I visit Joseph's grave?"

"Why not? We can go tomorrow. Let's meet at the Comboni Al-Majaneen at 10:00 in the morning."

"This sounds good. One last thing; is your mother here?"

"Yes, she's here."

"May I say hello to her?"

"Of course."

Osman called out, "Mama Mama!"

Fatima entered. She was a tall, dark-skinned woman with facial markings. Speaking in Dinka, she warmly greeted Anthony:

"Peace be upon you, my son."

Anthony replied, "Peace be upon you, Auntie," introducing himself.

"Are you from the Arumjok family?"

"Yes, Auntie. Do you know them?"

"Yes, they are the chiefs of our chieftaincy in Atokthou."

"Are you from Atokthou, Auntie?"

"Yes, I'm from the Patek clan, and my name is Abak Nuoi, but now I'm known as Fatima Nawai."

"Do you know Omda John Bak?" Anthony asked her.

"How could I not know him? Omda John Bak is my close relative."

"The late Joseph was his son."

She held Anthony's hand and wept bitterly. "Osman told me about Joseph's case, but I didn't know he was John Bak's son." She wept again.

"I'm sorry, Auntie. Life is unfair. May God have mercy on him and forgive him. I know your home now. I'll visit you again next time. See you, God willing." Anthony concluded, "Alright then, goodbye. See you tomorrow, Osman."

"Bye bye," Osman and his mother responded.

The following day, Osman met Anthony at Comboni, and together they went to the Muslim cemetery in Al-Sahafa to visit Joseph's grave. At the cemetery, Anthony promised Osman that the family would work to move the grave to a Christian cemetery, pending approval from the authorities. That was a request later denied by the local authorities.

19.

In mid-2002, the regime decided to sign the self-determination agreement for Southern Sudan with the Sudan People's Liberation Movement and the Sudan People's Liberation Army. A referendum was scheduled for the end of a six-year transitional period. A prominent figure in the government and the Islamic organisation, Ali Osman Taha, was assigned to lead the file in what was described as a serious step.

As part of the security arrangements, both parties agreed to establish a joint force to protect major cities and key figures. Among the 1,500 fighters sent from the Sudan People's Liberation Army to Khartoum was Yusuf Martin, who had killed Mohiy Al-Din Ahmed Sharif in Al-Imbab. He fled with his friend to Al-Ramila and then travelled the following morning to Southern Sudan via Kosti, where they joined the Sudan People's Liberation Army.

Furthermore, one of the agreed provisions in the Comprehensive Peace Agreement (CPA) included a general amnesty for fighters of the Sudan People's Liberation Army for politically motivated crimes committed against the state. Nevertheless, the amnesty did not extend to crimes of a personal nature. Yet, the family of the late Joseph John Bak agreed to close this case and refrain from raising the issue. They prayed for divine justice and for his soul to rest in peace. Still, narrating this story, as detailed in his will, became a promise to the living, a tale that had to be told for him to find eternal solace.

About the Author

Dr. Dhieu Mathok Diing Wol served as an Adjunct Associate Professor at the Center for Peace, Development Security Studies at Juba University.

He is currently the Minister of Investment and, at the same time, the Secretary of the Peace Mediation Committee addressing armed conflict in Sudan.

Dr. Wol was awarded the Peace Prize and named a Peace Ambassador by the Universal Peace Federation (UPF) for his role in mediating Sudanese conflict in 2020.

He has published numerous scholarly articles in

international journals specialising in peace studies, peace building and conflict resolution.

His published works by Al-Nokhba Publishing House:

Pastoralism, Boundaries and Disputes: Administration and Conflict Management in the 14-Mile Area

Politics of Ethnic Discrimination in Sudan

www.ingramcontent.com/pod-product-compliance
Lightning Source LLC
Chambersburg PA
CBHW011745020426
42333CB00022B/2720

DR. DHIEU MATHOK DIING WOL

There are countless stories, both personal and political, of tragedy an
horror, entwined in the relatively recent history of South Sudan, as
finds its way to independence.

Dr Dhieu Mathok Diing Wol, the current Minister of Investment in th
Revitalised Transitional Government, is an experienced and passionat
orator, recording the journeys of the people. A well-known ambassad
for peace, he has written about, and been extensively involved in peac
negotiations and conflict resolution.

Taking a different genre, in this story he has written an account o
mistaken identity, the result of which caused a family and a communit
unspeakable heartbreak. We all know how it feels to lose a loved one, bu
when the reason for the loss is undeniably the fault of another, it canno
go unspoken. Dr Wol took up the challenge of putting the recor
straight, for the family of Joseph John Bak.

The excellent Introduction, written by publisher Osama Ibrahin
applauds Dr Wol's skilful integration of political dynamics into the dai
life of the people through this personal story.

The story can be read on several levels. It is a tale of injustice, and also o
love and acceptance, of Muslims protecting Christians, and of the histor
of this turbulent time. Above all, it is hoped that this will help to lay t
rest the anger and despair of one man's family, forced to come to term
with the wrongful death of their loved one, Joseph.

ISBN 978-1-7638734-6-9

Africa
World Books
Pty Ltd

9 781763 873469

RAW FOOD

YOUR GUIDE & COOKBOOK TO A HEALTHY RAW FOOD DIET

2ND EDITION

NICO SMART